The View from Saturday

E. L. Konigsburg

TEACHER GUIDE

NOTE:

The trade book edition of the novel used to prepare this guide is found in the Novel Units catalog and on the Novel Units website. Using other editions may have varied page references.

Please note: We have assigned Interest Levels based on our knowledge of the themes and ideas of the books included in the Novel Units sets, however, please assess the appropriateness of this novel or trade book for the age level and maturity of your students prior to reading with them. You know your students best!

ISBN 978-1-56137-935-4

To order, contact your local school supply store, or:

Toll-Free Fax: 877.716.7272
Phone: 888.650.4224
3901 Union Blvd., Suite 155
St. Louis, MO 63115

sales@novelunits.com

novelunits.com

Table of Contents

Skills and Strategies

Thinking
    Brainstorming, research

Literary Elements
    Story elements, simile/
    metaphor, characterization,
    framework story, humor,
    personification, symbol,
    dialogue, theme

Listening/Speaking
    Interviewing, role play

Comprehension
    Predicting, comparison/
    contrast

Writing
    Reading response log,
    letters, creative, narrative,
    persuasive

Vocabulary
    Synonyms, antonyms, word
    mapping, sorting

Summary of *The View from Saturday*

Four students, with their own individual stories, develop a special bond and attract the attention of their teacher, a paraplegic, who chooses them to represent their sixth grade class in the Academic Bowl competition. The plot is composed of interwoven puzzles. What prompts Mrs. Olinski to choose Noah, Nadia, Ethan, and Julian for the team over the usual overachievers and honor students in her class? What do they know about her, themselves, and each other that gives them the advantage? Each has a tale to tell, in the course of which all four witness acts of kindness and respect that teach them to find those feelings in themselves and others.

About the Author

Elaine Lobl Konigsburg was born in New York, N.Y. in 1930. She did most of her growing up in a small town in Pennsylvania. She studied to be a scientist and was a science teacher in Florida before she married. She has three children. She found that writing stories was more fun than working as a scientist. When her children started school, she decided to write a book about what was happening to them in their school and community. She has said, "All my stories use the same things in different proportions: things that happen to me, to my family, to my friends, things that I read, that I see, that I hear about. When I stir all this together and write it down, the people become characters..." (Commire, Anne [editor]. *Something About the Author*, page 137. Detroit: Gale Research, 1985.)

Other writings by E. L. Konigsburg are:

About the B'nai Bagels
Altogether, One at a Time
From the Mixed-up Files of Mrs. Basil E. Frankweiler
(George)
Jennifer, Hecate, Macbeth, William McKinley, and Me, Elizabeth
Journey to an 800 Number
A Proud Taste for Scarlet and Miniver
Samuel Todd's Book of Great Colors
Samuel Todd's Book of Great Inventions
The Second Mrs. Giaconda
T-Backs, T-Shirts, Coat, and Suit
Throwing Shadows
Up from Jericho Tel

Introductory Activities and Information

Note:
It is not intended that everything presented in this guide be done. Please be selective and use discretion when choosing the activities you will do with the unit. The choices that are made should be appropriate for your use and your group of students. A wide range of activities has been provided so that individuals as well as groups may benefit.

1. Prediction: Have students examine the cover illustration and title, then flip through the book. Ask: What kind of book do you suppose this will be? What is suggested by the title?

2. Reviews and Summary: Read aloud the remarks on the back cover and the back cover summary. Ask: What does the back cover summary tell you about what to expect from this book? (At this point, you might want to provide the author background from page 3 of this guide.)

3. Prereading Discussion Topics: Encourage free, open-ended discussion on these topics, or use them as writing assignments.

   Grandparents: What images come to mind when you hear the word "grandparent"? Have you ever been surprised to find out someone was a grandparent when he/she didn't look "old enough" to be one? How do grandparents often help their children and grandchildren, especially in single-parent situations? As grandparents age, what kinds of problems sometimes develop? What advantages are there for senior citizens in retirement villages? How do retirement villages differ from nursing homes?

   Aging: Unless you die young, you too will be "old" someday. Do you find it difficult to imagine yourself as a "senior citizen"? What activities do you hope will still be part of your life when you are 80? What kind of music will you be listening to? How will you dress?

   Friends: What are some characteristics of people you consider to be your closest friends? Have you ever been forced to spend time with someone you didn't expect to like—but then found to be a friend? What does it take to be a good friend to someone? Should friends always be honest with one another?

   Marriage: Why do people get married? What do you think are the ingredients of a good marriage? What should a woman "look for" in a potential husband? Are these the same qualities a man should look for in the woman he is considering marrying?

Handicapped: What does this word mean? What kinds of handicaps are there? How do handicapped people cope with their special problems? How can others help the handicapped in the work place? Have you ever had a handicapped teacher?

4. Log: Have students keep a response log as they read.

In one type of log, the student pretends to be one of the characters. Writing on one side of each piece of paper, the student writes in the first person ("I...") about his/her reaction to what happened in that chapter. A partner responds to these writings on the other side of the paper, as if talking to the character.

In the dual entry log, students jot down brief summaries and reactions to each section of the novel they have read. (The first entry could be made based on a preview of the novel—a glance at the cover and a flip through the book.)

Pages	Summary	Reactions
		(These might begin: "I liked the part where Noah and his mother discuss the B&B letter...", "This reminded me of the time I...", "If I were Noah's mother, would...")

In a third type of log, students choose a passage from each section that strikes them for some reason, copy it, and explain why the passage seems important to them. (Has the author used language in a special way? created beautiful word pictures? expressed an important insight? raised a question in the reader's mind? somehow brought to mind something in the reader's life?)

In the fourth type of log, students divide the page into three columns and respond to the story in three ways:

-comments/questions for the characters
-comments/questions for the author
-comments about the reader's personal reactions to the story

Alternatively, as students read, they might simply jot thoughts and questions on sticky notes and apply them to the passage in question for later reference.

5

5. Writing: Have students freewrite for ten minutes using one of the following "starters."

- On Saturdays I like to...
- Grandparents are...
- Scholastic competitions...
- Weddings involve...
- Girls and boys can be on the same teams when...

Vocabulary Activities

1. For each reading section, have students choose five to seven words whose definitions they don't know. Then let them choose from several activities to "journal" each word:

A. Word Triangle   B. Word Bug

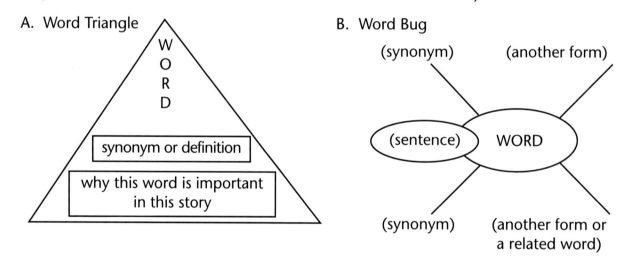

C. Word Card

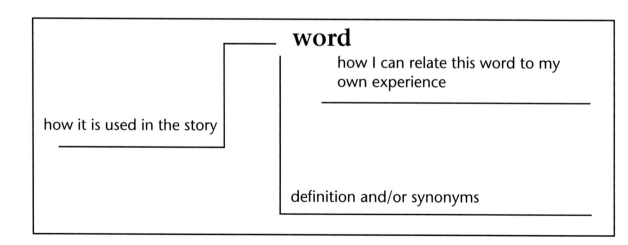

2. Have students use a software program or graph paper to create crossword puzzles and clues for a specific list of words from one or two reading sections. Have them trade their puzzles for solving.

3. Word Sort: Present students with target words.

   Divide students into cooperative groups and have them sort the words into categories. (A word might go into more than one category.) A representative from each group explains the sortings to the whole class, and differences between group decisions are discussed. Categories:

   <u>Words that Describe</u>

   Plants   Animals   Humans   Places   Activities

4. Synonym Trains: Have students work together to create "synonym trains" and "antonym trains."

   SYNONYMS—
   Example: **DIN**—NOISE—UPROAR—TUMULT—

   ANTONYMS—
   Example: **VIVID**—FORGETTABLE—COLORLESS—BLAND—

5. Vocabulary Log: Students keep a log of important vocabulary words (selected either by them or by you) that they meet in the story, context clues (if any), and the definition for some, but not all, of the words on the list. (Requiring students to look up every unfamiliar word is not advisable; it can be an overwhelming task.)

Word	Clues to meaning	Dictionary Definition

6. Definitions: Have students play the "Definition Game" with selected vocabulary words.

   Players sit in a circle. The player who is "up" looks up the word in a dictionary and reads the definition (keeping the page out of the other players' view). The winner is the student who guesses the most words which match the definitions. (You might decide to have students give guesses in turn to avoid a free-for-all.)

7. Mobiles: Make word mobiles using several vocabulary words related to one idea. For each word, include the pronunciation from the dictionary, the location of the word in the book, how you'd use it in your everyday language, as well as a working definition.

8. Pantomime: Have students act out some of the vocabulary words and see if classmates can guess the target words.

9. Vocabulary Password: Students play in pairs, one giving the definition and the other answering. Definition-giver gets a list of words to try to get his/her partner to say. The pair of students who can guess the most words in a specified number of minutes wins.

10. Trivial Pursuit: Use a "Trivial Pursuit" board with vocabulary words and definitions on 3 x 5 cards for each category. Players must give the word for the definition which is read aloud to score.

11. Complete the Vocabulary Puzzle Page on the next page of this guide.

Vocabulary Puzzle Page

Directions: Fill in each puzzle piece with as many words as possible found in the vocabulary of the entire novel.

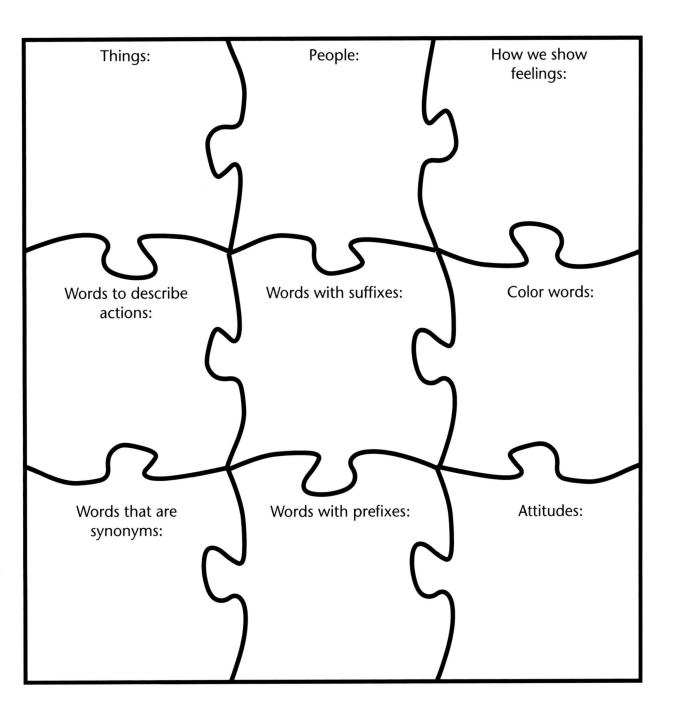

Things:

People:

How we show feelings:

Words to describe actions:

Words with suffixes:

Color words:

Words that are synonyms:

Words with prefixes:

Attitudes:

Using Predictions in the Novel Unit Approach

We all make predictions as we read—little guesses about what will happen next, how the conflict will be resolved, which details given by the author will be important to the plot, which details will help to fill in our sense of a character. Students should be encouraged to predict, to make sensible guesses. As students work on predictions, these discussion questions can be used to guide them: What are some of the ways to predict? What is the process of a sophisticated reader's thinking and predicting? What clues does an author give us to help us in making our predictions? Why are some predictions more likely than others?

A predicting chart is for students to record their predictions. As each subsequent chapter is discussed, you can review and correct previous predictions. This procedure serves to focus on predictions and to review the stories.

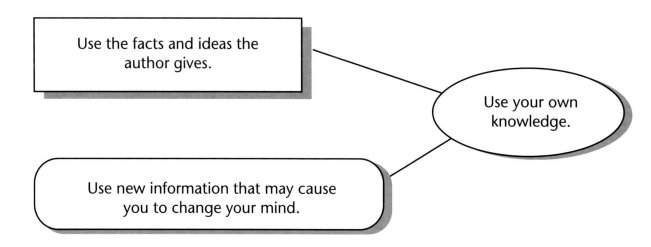

Prediction Chart

What characters have we met so far?	What is the conflict in the story?	What are your predictions?	Why did you make those predictions?

Story Map

Setting

⬇

Problem

⬇

Goal

⬇

Episodes

⬇

Resolution

Characters_____

_____

_____

_____

Time and Place_____

_____

_____

_____

Beginning ⟶ Development ⟶ Outcome

_____

_____

_____

_____

_____

_____

_____

Using Character Webs—In the Novel Unit Approach

Attribute Webs are simply a visual representation of a character from the novel. They provide a systematic way for the students to organize and recap the information they have about a particular character. Attribute webs may be used after reading the novel to recapitulate information about a particular character or completed gradually as information unfolds, done individually, or finished as a group project.

One type of character attribute web uses these divisions:

- How a character acts and feels. (How does the character feel in this picture? How would you feel if this happened to you? How do you think the character feels?)

- How a character looks. (Close your eyes and picture the character. Describe him to me.)

- Where a character lives. (Where and when does the character live?)

- How others feel about the character. (How does another specific character feel about our character?)

In group discussion about the student attribute webs and specific characters, the teacher can ask for backup proof from the novel. You can also include inferential thinking.

Attribute webs need not be confined to characters. They may also be used to organize information about a concept, object or place.

Attribute Web

The attribute web below is designed to help you gather clues the author provides about what a character is like. Fill in the blanks with words and phrases which tell how the character acts and looks, as well as what the character says and what others say about him or her.

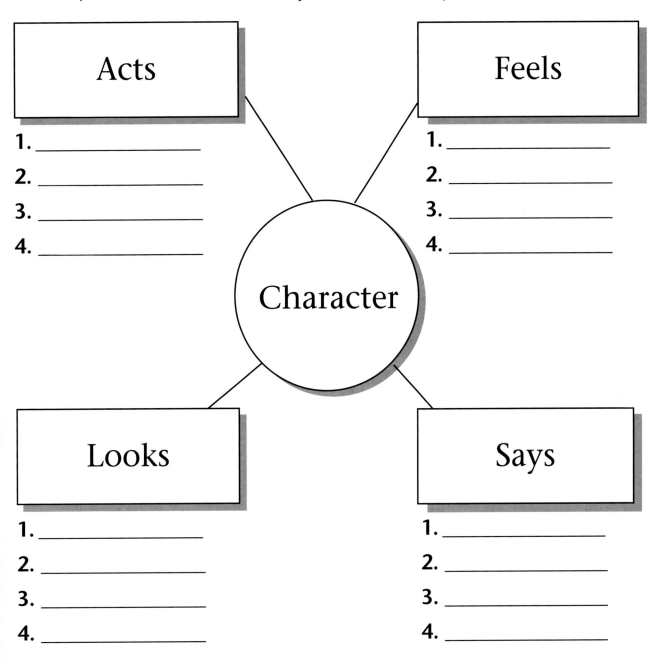

Acts
1. _____
2. _____
3. _____
4. _____

Feels
1. _____
2. _____
3. _____
4. _____

Character

Looks
1. _____
2. _____
3. _____
4. _____

Says
1. _____
2. _____
3. _____
4. _____

13

Attribute Web

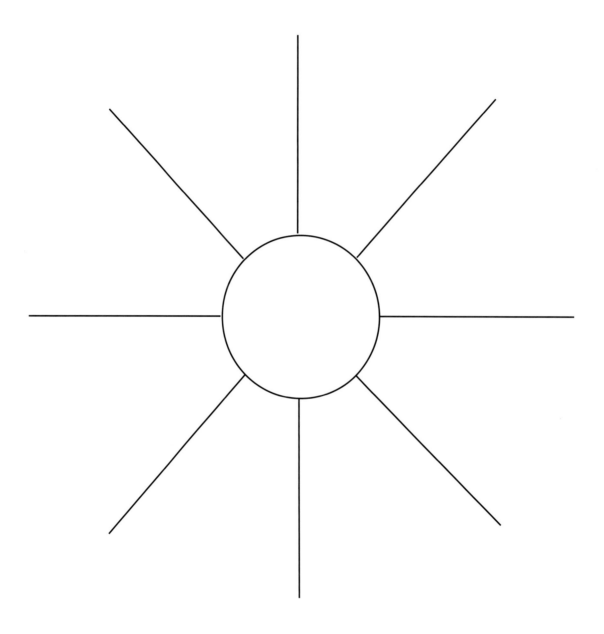

Chapter-by-Chapter Vocabulary, Discussion Questions, and Activities

Chapter 1—Pages 1-20

Chapter Opening Summary—Pages 1-4:
Mrs. Olinski remembers the answers she has given for her choice of team members for the Academic Bowl. She thinks about why The Souls are truly a team and how unusual it is that sixth graders have made it to the finals.

"Noah Writes a B & B Letter"—Pages 5-20
Noah remembers the wedding he had played a part in as he writes his B & B letter.

Vocabulary:

benevolently 3	baited breath 3	calligraphy 4	destinations 7
nibs 9	domiciles 10	version 11	maimed 15

Discussion Questions and Activities:

1. What is the setting—time and place—in which the story opens on pages 1-4? What is the setting on pages 5-20? *(Page 1, The story opens on Academic Bowl day in Albany, New York. The setting for page 5 is New York State, but Noah is remembering his trip to Florida.)*

2. What is a B & B letter? *(Page 5, A "bread and butter" letter is one that you write to people to thank them for having you as their houseguest.)* Why did Noah think his mother, not he, should be sending the thank you letter? *(Pages 5-6, His mother was able to go on a cruise she had won because the grandparents cared for the children.)*

3. What are your impressions of Noah? *(Pages 5-6, He is a bit of a smarty but restrains himself with his mother. Noah is also imaginative and innovative.)* How does Noah demonstrate his creativeness and imagination? *(pages 11 and 18, cat paw invitations and surprise gifts)* How does his mother handle him and get him to do what she wants? How would your mother talk to Noah?

4. What was the biggest event in Noah's visit to Florida? *(Pages 10-19, He helped prepare for a wedding of senior citizens at the retirement village.)* What were the high points that Noah remembered? Why were Post-It notes, a calligraphy pen and ink, a tuxedo T-shirt and a red wagon important?

5. How was Noah helpful? *(He wrote the invitations and helped run the organizing of coupons for the wedding dinner. When Allen, the best man, was injured, Noah stepped right into the best man's place with a painted tuxedo. He helped move the*

wedding cake and also helped with the delivery of flowers.) Would the senior citizens have been able to manage the wedding without him?

6. How do you think senior citizens would react to Noah's definition of the retirement center as a place where old people lived who had "retired from useful life"? (page 7) How would you describe a retirement village?

7. Do you think Noah found that being around the old people was boring? Why or why not? What did the old people do to help the situation? *(Pages 10-19, They gave Noah something to do and made him feel a part of the important event.)*

8. What does *ironic* mean? *(page 13, "the contrast between what you expect to happen and what really happens")* Why did Noah think it was ironic that Allen Diamondstein should say that the red wagon was the problem? (page 15)

9. What superstitions might people have thought about if they knew the fate of the couple on the top of the toppled wedding cake? (page 15)

10. Which part of the chapter did you find funniest? Do you think the characters saw the humor?

Supplementary Activities:

1. Literary Analysis—Framework Story: A framework story is a story within a story. The framework may or may not have a plot itself, and the story may or may not return to the frame situation at the end. Mrs. Olinski and the Academic Bowl provide a frame for the stories of the four contestants.

   A story map is an outline that helps you to understand and remember the story better. Because this is a framework story, it is harder to make a story line diagram. Begin the story map on page 17 of this guide. As the story is read, more characters may be added and the setting and the problem may change, so additions to the story map may be made. You may want to make story maps for each of the chapters on Noah, Nadia, Ethan and Julian, plus the overall map of the entire book.

Story Map

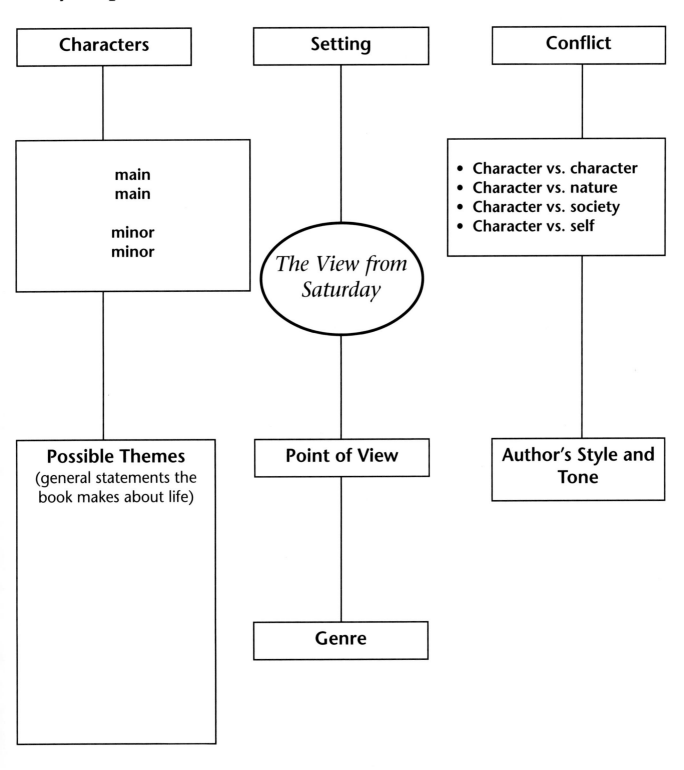

Characters

main
main

minor
minor

Setting

The View from Saturday

Conflict

- Character vs. character
- Character vs. nature
- Character vs. society
- Character vs. self

Possible Themes
(general statements the book makes about life)

Point of View

Author's Style and Tone

Genre

2. Literary Analysis—Characterization: Explain that characterization is the way an author informs readers about what characters are like. Direct characterization is when the author describes the character. Indirect characterization is when the reader figures out what the character is like based on what the character thinks, says, or does—or what other characters say about him or her.

Ask: "What are your impressions of Noah so far?" Ask students to support any words or phrases they use to describe Noah with evidence from the story. Have them jot down the evidence on a web like this one. For each of the major characters in this novel, make a character web.

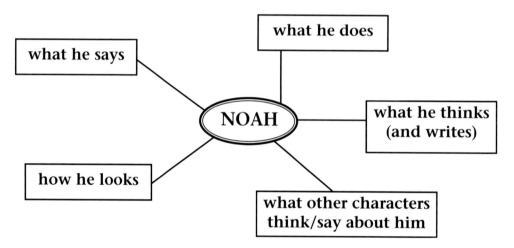

3. Literary Analysis—Humor:
    1. Can you list five things that kids think are funny but adults do not?
    2. What are all the ways adults are funnier than kids?
    3. Why are some people funnier than others?
    4. What is a practical joke? What is the difference between a funny practical joke and a mean joke?
    5. Would you rather see something funny or hear something funny? Why?
    6. Is it better to laugh at someone or be the one laughed at? Does laughter ever hurt?
    7. What comes after a funny joke?

Write your definition of humor.

4. Research: How many retirement communities are in your area? What opportunities do they provide for interaction with young people? Do they invite young people for Christmas programs or provide any tutoring help to children? What can young people learn from senior citizens?

5. Writing Ideas:
   1. Write Noah's B & B thank you letter.
   2. How could events in Noah's story have been changed to create a different ending? Write another version of Noah's story.
   3. Noah was inventive. As you read the novel, find other examples of courage and inventiveness. Would you rather be courageous or inventive? Write a short paper with examples from your life.

6. Interview: Interview a grandparent or other older person in your family or neighborhood. Find out how things have changed. Does your interviewee think the "old days" were better than present times? What are his or her happiest memories? saddest?

Chapter 2—Pages 21-57

Chapter Opening Summary—Pages 21-24:
At the Academic Bowl contest, Mrs. Olinski thinks about the superintendent and her answer to why she had chosen the members of the team. Mrs. Olinski sees Nadia as a beautiful person with a cautious, friendly manner.

"Nadia Tells of Turtle Love"—Pages 25-57
Nadia describes her vacation with her father and grandparents in Florida. These are the grandparents who were married with the assistance of Noah. Nadia has adjustment problems with her divorced father and her move to New York. She compares the turtles commuting up and down the Atlantic with her joint custody and vacations between New York and Florida. She no longer feels comfortable with her Florida friends in the old neighborhood. She had enjoyed working with her grandfather and Margaret before they were married. The fun of moving turtle nests and saving the turtles has changed and she is uncomfortable with Ethan, Margaret's grandson, until the northeaster hits and she swallows her resentment and jealousy and helps save the turtles.

Vocabulary:

podium 21	onyx 21	coiffed 21	incandescently 24
de facto 25	mixed marriage 26	hovered 26	bubbe 26
atrociously 27	zaftig 27	prepubescent 27	unforeseen 28
gourmet 32	tranquilize 35	hybridization 36	thoroughbred 36
ruggelach 39	bobka 39	subtle 40	recipient 47
communicator 48	sarcasm 49	pathetic 51	frazzled 51
philosophical 54	frenzy 54		

Discussion Questions and Activities:

1. The story returns to Mrs. Olinski and the championship contest and the question of why she chose the contest participants for the team. What was her response to the question? *(page 22, diversity)* How do you know she was joking? *(Page 22, She said "I chose a brunette, a redhead, a blond, and a kid with hair as black as newsprint.")* Do you think that Dr. Rohmer has a sense of humor? How would you define a sense of humor?

2. What did Mrs. Olinski mean by "the word (cripple) itself does not hurt, but the manner of its delivery can"? *(page 23)* Give some other examples of words that can hurt.

3. How are Mrs. Olinski and Nadia alike? *(Page 23, Both "seemed most disconnected. Both were watchers and waiters, cautious about being friendly, about showing themselves.")* Why are they both cautious? What are they afraid of?

4. What are Nadia's major problems on her vacation time with her father? *(Page 26, He no longer knows how to treat her, he hovers and he is so nervous.)* What is a mixed marriage? *(page 26, a marriage between two people of different religions, racial or ethnic backgrounds)* What does a divorce settlement have to do with how much time Nadia spends with her father? *(Page 25, The amount of time that the parents spend with each child is a part of the divorce settlement, as well as how much each parent must pay for the care of the child.)* Why does her father "hover" over her? Why do you think he does it, and why does Nadia resent it? Do you think Nadia is more like her mother or her father? Do you have any basis on which to judge this?

5. Why are the turtles important in this chapter? How do turtles bring all the characters in this chapter together? How is the turtle a symbol? What does the turtle represent? How did Nadia learn so much about them? How had turtles brought Grandpa Izzy and Margaret together? Why do you think Nadia's father became involved with the turtle walk? Why do you think he wanted to be "permitted"?

6. How does Nadia compare her mother's return to New York to the turtle migration patterns? *(Page 39, "…I wondered if her need to return to autumn in New York had anything to do with some switch that had been turned on when she emerged.")*

7. How did Nadia show that she was jealous and lonely? *(Pages 42-43, Margaret with her loggerhead turtles had gotten Grandpa and now Nadia's father who wanted to be "permitted." Page 47, Nadia refused to go to the condo or to the turtle walk.)* What did Nadia mean: "Inside me was a lot of best friendship that no one but Ginger was using"? *(Pages 29, 42-43, She no longer felt comfortable with her friends in her old neighborhood, she did not feel that Grandpa and Margaret were close to her or as much fun as they had been, and she really did not enjoy Ethan.)*

8. Why was Nadia so impatient and angry with Ethan? *(Pages 44-47, He knew that his grandmother [Margaret] had arranged an interview and job opportunity for Nadia's mother in New York. Everyone had known this except Nadia, and now she was the one who had to commute between New York and Florida. She blamed Margaret for her mother leaving her father and the move to New York.)*

9. How did the information about her mother's job change Nadia's activities in Florida? *(Page 47, She thought Margaret had interfered with her life and so she wanted nothing more to do with her—no more walking on the beach, no more swimming and breakfast, and no more turtle walks.)* How did Nadia tell her father that she wanted nothing to do with Margaret and really him? Do you think that Margaret thought she was interfering? How could Nadia have discussed this situation with her father?

10. How did the northeaster help Nadia, her father and the grandparents? *(Page 55, Nadia realized her personal anger and disappointments were not as important as helping the turtles.)* How did Nadia compare her father's problems with the turtles? *(Page 55, "The storm in our private lives had picked him up and put him out of place.")* What do you think Nadia's father meant when he said, "And there will be times when you or I will need a lift between switches"? (page 57)

Supplementary Activities:

1. Literary Analysis—Simile and Metaphor: A simile is a figure of speech in which a similarity between two essentially unlike objects is directly expressed, using the words "like" or "as." For example, on page 23, "...she [Nadia] was as plump as a perfectly ripened peach." How is Nadia like a peach? *(Nadia has red hair and is pleasantly plump like a well-ripened peach.)* Why is this an apt comparison?

   A metaphor does not use any extra words. It simply says something is something else. For example: *John is the tower of strength.*

2. Literary Analysis—Symbol: A symbol is an object, character, or incident that stands for something else. In literature, writers often use everyday objects as ideas to represent something of greater significance. Have students name a symbol in the novel (i.e., the turtles) and explain its importance.

3. Writing:
   • If you could only save one endangered animal, which animal would it be? Why?
   • Some people might like New York State more than Florida. What are some of the reasons? Which state do you think Nadia prefers? Why?

- Write a letter from Nadia to an advice columnist and write her response. What do you think are some of the problems Nadia might seek help with?
- Write your own similes to replace some of these:

  Page 26, "...Dad hovered over me like the Goodyear blimp over the Orange Bowl."

  Page 26, "...Grandpa Izzy's eyes are bright blue like the sudden underside of a bird wing."

  Page 128, "...lifted their thumbs like a forest of small apostrophes at the ends of their closed fists."

4. Use a Venn diagram to show how Nadia and Mrs. Olinski are alike.

5. Complete the Dialogue Page on the next page of this guide.

6. Research turtle migratory patterns. See the Teacher Information section of this guide.

7. Role play other ways that Nadia could have discussed handling Margaret's interference.

Chapter 3—Pages 58-93

Chapter Opening Summary—Pages 58-60:
Mrs. Olinski fills in the background of Margaret Draper and her grandson, Ethan. Margaret Draper had been a very good teacher and was Mrs. Olinski's demanding principal before the accident that killed her husband and in which she lost the use of her legs. Mrs. Olinski chose Ethan for the team, not because he was Margaret Draper's grandson but because he was bright and had the "right" kind of attitude.

"Ethan Explains the B and B Inn"—Pages 61-93
Ethan tells the story of how he met Julian, the negative impressions he made, the invitation to tea, and the beginning of The Souls.

Vocabulary:
unruly 61	nonchalantly 61	suffragette 62	archive 62
trestle 65	inevitable 68	alien 85	incubating 93

Discussion Questions and Activities:
1. Margaret Draper thought kids had changed. What example did she give? *(Page 59, "Sixth graders had stopped asking 'Now what?' and had started asking 'So what?' ")* Do you think sixth graders have really changed in the last twenty five or thirty years? If so, why? How does Ethan differ from the typical sixth grader? Can you explain this? Why do you think Mrs. Olinski picked Ethan as part of the team?

Using Dialogue

Directions: Choose a bit of dialogue from the book to investigate. Fill in the chart to describe this way of writing and telling a story.

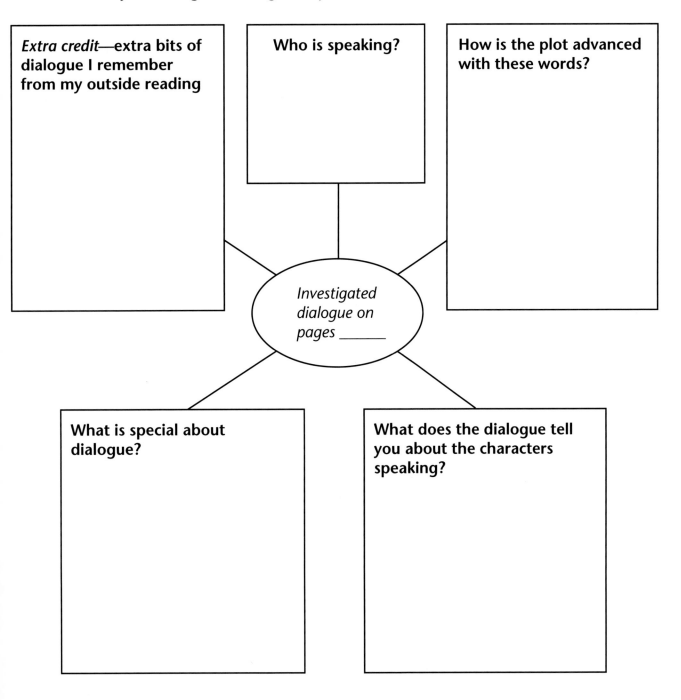

Extra credit—extra bits of dialogue I remember from my outside reading

Who is speaking?

How is the plot advanced with these words?

Investigated dialogue on pages _____

What is special about dialogue?

What does the dialogue tell you about the characters speaking?

2. Ethan has an older brother. How is this brother a problem? *(Page 63, Luke, the brother, is very bright, and every teacher expects Ethan to be a genius also.)* Do you think Ethan's parents have compared the boys? How could this affect Ethan? How should parents treat siblings with different talents and abilities? What do Ethan's parents do for a living? *(Page 63, They are farmers.)* What do they expect him to do when he grows up? *(Page 74, He will inherit the farm.)* What does Ethan really want? *(Page 74, He wants to go to New York and design costumes or stage sets for plays.)*

3. How do the people who live in The Farm (Them) differ from Ethan's family, the farmers (Us)? *(pages 63-64)* Use a T-diagram to show the differences.

Them	Us
Farming is a lifestyle.	Farming is a livelihood.
How They look at milk—recycled grass	Milk comes from cows.
How They look at dirt—dirt gets no respect	Dirt is the working layer of the earth, necessary to work with, and a part of farm life

4. How did Julian manage to do all the wrong things? *(Page 66, He introduces himself, shakes hands, wears shorts and knee socks and carries a leather book bag.)* What is the acceptable look in this school? Who can get away with wearing really different clothes or not acting like everyone else in your school? The kids went out of their way to make Julian's life miserable. Why do you think Ethan decided to stand up for Julian? What characteristics did Julian exhibit when he changed the sign on his book bag?

5. What kind of relationship did Ethan and Julian have? *(Pages 76-77, They did not talk on the bus even though they shared a seat. Ethan stood up for Julian against the bullies in the class.)* Why was the invitation to the tea party unusual? Was it necessary to bring a present if it was not a birthday? What type of present would you bring to an unusual boy like Julian? How would you react if one of your friends gave you a big pink heart puzzle wrapped in pink paper? Why isn't this appropriate for a sixth grade boy? Was Julian offended? Why or why not?

6. Ethan used the words "neat" and "awesome" in conversation. (page 82) He knew he should have said something beside these overused words. What would you have said? Nadia's gift of Alice, the puppy, was a bit presumptuous. How would your parents react if you received a present of a dog?

7. What did Julian mean when he said, "I am as American as pizza pie. I did not originate here, but I am here to stay." *(Page 85, Pizza is an Italian food, but Americans really like it and eat so much of it that it seems to have become a staple in the American diet.)* What is an alien? Explain why Julian's birth on the high seas made him an American citizen.

8. Ethan was thinking about the tea party at Sillington House. What do you think he meant by, "Had I gained something at Sillington House? Or had I lost something there? The answer was yes"? (page 89) What do you think Ethan gained and lost?

9. How did the group choose their name, "The Souls"? *(Page 90, Nadia won the prize of picking a name for the group by pulling off the longest strip of wallpaper.)* Do you have a group of friends that gets together regularly? Do you have a name? What kind of activities do you plan? What do you usually do on Saturday afternoons?

10. What do you think Nadia meant when she said, "Noah Gershom, you may be smart beyond your years, but you are not wise"? (page 90) As a first step in your explanation, make a list of synonyms for the words *smart* and *wise*. Using this list, discuss your answers.

11. If you had a chance to live over one day, which day would you choose?

12. Julian has talent as a magician. What is this talent called? *(page 93, chops)* Find examples in the novel as you read.

13. How has Ethan changed because of The Souls? *(Page 93, He talks more and has more confidence.)* Notice the other characters. Do they change in the novel?

Prediction:
How will the shiny new pennies be used?

Supplementary Activities:
1. Begin the Literary Analysis Chart on the next page of this guide.

2. Writing:
   • Make a list of what ordinary kids would do on Saturday afternoon instead of tea parties. Make a list of the activities of your group of friends for last weekend. Will the activities differ with the seasons and the area of the country?

   • Pick any character in the story and tell why you think that character is the funniest, most likable, bravest, least likable, friendliest, most adventurous, most troublesome or mischievous, etc.

3. Research the minting of coins. How could we get brand new pennies? Where are they made? What is on the front and back of the penny? Do you think pennies should be abolished? Could we get along without them?

Literary Analysis Chart

Directions: One way authors let us know what characters are like is by showing us how they interact with other characters. On the "spokes" surrounding each character's name, write several adjectives that describe that character. On the arrows joining Mrs. Olinski to the other characters, write descriptions of their relationships. (How does Mrs. Olinski feel and act toward each person? How does each of them feel and act toward her?)

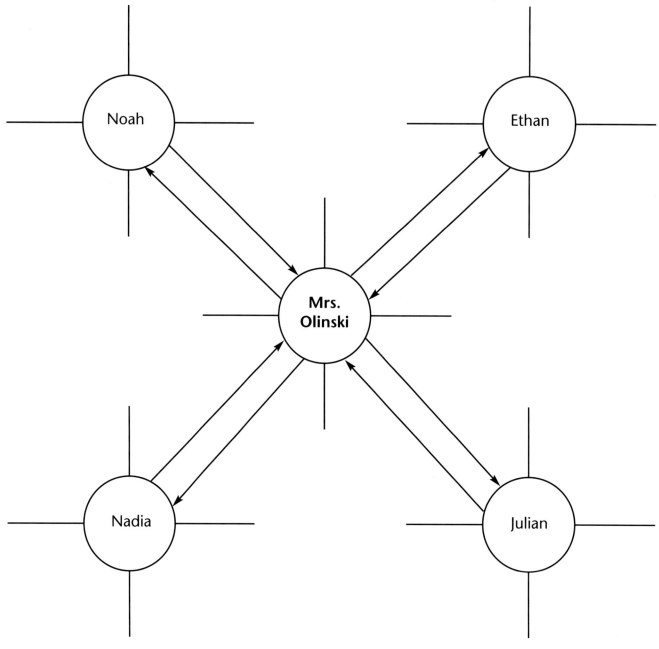

Chapter 4—Pages 94-118

Chapter Opening Summary—Pages 94-98:

Mrs. Olinski remembers introducing herself to her sixth grade class and Hamilton Knapp's response to her writing on the lower half of the board. She recalls another rude applause response probably started by Hamilton and his friends. The Souls decide that they will give Mrs. Olinski their support against the troublesome sixth graders.

"Julian Narrates When Ginger Played Annie's Sandy"—Pages 99-118

Nadia's dog Ginger wins a role in the high school play, *Annie*. Michael Froelich's dog, Arnold, is the understudy. Jared Lord and Hamilton Knapp plan to embarrass Ginger and Nadia by substituting laxatives and tranquilizers for dog treats, but Arnold unexpectedly is asked to play the part and would have caused lots of trouble if Julian had not discovered what the two boys planned to do. Julian is tempted to allow Arnold to eat the drugged treats, but he switches them. After the play Julian uses his magic tricks to let Hamilton and his mother know about the drugged biscuits. Knapp and Lord also set up a disturbance at the play.

Vocabulary:

spontaneous 96	suppressed 96	admonish 96	canine 99
bickering 101	palm a treat 102	tamping 110	

Discussion Questions and Activities:

1. Why did The Souls decide to help Mrs. Olinski? *(Page 97, They believed that some of their classmates were exceptionally rude to her.)* What do the expressions "Stand on her own two feet" and "you don't have a leg to stand on" mean? What kind of a "lift" could The Souls give Mrs. Olinski?

2. How does Ethan behave differently when he is with The Souls? Why? *(Pages 104-105, He is a very quiet boy who lacks confidence. When he is with The Souls he knows he can do better.)*

3. Give an example to show what the author meant by, "Second best can be worse than not-in-the-running." (page 105)

4. How did Julian learn of the plot to embarrass Ginger and Nadia? *(Pages 107-108, He overheard Jared Lord and Ham Knapp talking about tranquilizers and doggie treats.)* How did Julian get the word to the other Souls? *(Page 109, He passed the Year-of-The-Souls penny to them.)* How did Arnold get the opportunity to star in the play on Friday? *(Page 111, He had come to all the practices.)*

5. Why did the students join in with Knapp and Lord in the bad theater behavior? *(Page 114, It is easier to go along with the group.)* What could you do in such a situation? What characteristics do you have to have to refuse to go along with the group or to stand up for what is right?

6. Why do you think Julian made the decision to prevent Arnold from eating the drugged treats? What adjectives describe Julian's decision?

7. How did Julian violate the teachings about magic he learned from Gopal?
(Pages 117-118, He revealed some of his secret by pulling doggie treats out of Ham's ears and dropping the rest of the drugged treats into his lap.)

Supplementary Activities:
1. The switch back and forth in time in the sections of this novel is sometimes confusing. Make a time chart.

2. Research how handicapped vans work.

3. Complete the Decision-making Grid on the next page of this guide.

Chapters 5 & 6—Pages 119-131

Chapter 5 Summary:
Mrs. Olinski thinks about who she wants for the sixth grade contestants. She eliminates Hamilton Knapp after she watches his behavior when Mrs. Reynolds scolds the audience after the play. The Souls, Margy, and Izzy meet for tea at Sillington House, and Mrs. Olinski notes how courteous and cooperative her students are. Then she makes up her mind about the sixth grade academic team.

Chapter 6 Summary:
The Souls academic team wins several rounds and they look like strong contestants. Ham and Jared misbehave by belching in Mrs. Olinski's class and she calls them before the class.

Vocabulary:

dictatorial 119	waffled 120	tolerance 121	malice 121
vulgar 123	animated 125	trounce 127	profound 127
mediocre 127	culled 127	vanquished 128	flanks 128
trajectory 129	jubilant 131		

Discussion Questions and Activities:
1. What do you think Mrs. Olinski meant when she said, "...sometimes to be successful, you have to risk making mistakes," and, "...sometimes we even have to risk making fools of ourselves"? (pages 119-120) Give examples from your life that will justify what you believe.

2. "Mrs. Olinski had a great tolerance for mischief, but she had no patience for malice." (page 121) How does mischief differ from pranks of malice? Give some examples.

Decision-making Grid

The decision-making grid below is supposed to make it easier to find the best solution to a problem. Give examples of other questions you should ask yourself when you are trying to "weigh" different solutions. Then fill in the grid for the following problem: *My best friend has been telling lies about me.* See if classmates agree with the solution you decide is best.

Problem	Criterion #1	Criterion #2	Criterion #3
State the problem.	Will the solution hurt someone?	Will it make me feel better?	
Solution #1			
Solution #2			
Solution #3			
Solution #4			

3. Why might Mrs. Olinski feel jealousy, injury, or anger when she looked at Margy being greeted by the students who had participated in her wedding? (page 124)

4. What does the reference to David versus Goliath mean? slingshots? *(Page 128, In the Bible, the boy David slays the giant Philistine Goliath with a slingshot.)*

5. Mrs. Olinski called Ham and Jared to the front of the room to teach the class how to belch on command. She said, "...the only tricks that I am willing to put up with are those that you can first explain and then teach." (page 130) Do you think that this kind of punishment would work in Mrs. Olinski's class and help keep them in line? What other kinds of punishment would you suggest to Mrs. Olinski?

Supplementary Activities:
1. Writing: Intuition is knowing something without any particular reason for knowing it. Which character in this novel is the most intuitive? Support your choice with some examples.

2. Would you rather have a job that paid big money but you really hated, or a job that paid very little but you really loved? How would Mrs. Olinski answer this question? How do you know?

3. List your ideas about cooperation.

4. Complete the Characterization-Reaction Chart on page 31 of this guide.

Chapters 7 & 8—Pages 132-145

Chapter 7 Summary:
Julian on two occasions differs with the commissioner and the deputy superintendent. On both occasions he is respectful but he could have caused trouble for the successful Souls. The principal of Knightsbridge School tells Mrs. Olinski that his team better win because he has told his sixth grade coach that she will be hung if their team is beaten by The Souls. This is the beginning of the symbol of the piece of rope. The Souls win the contest and they carry Mrs. Olinski and the wheelchair on their shoulders.

Chapter 8 Summary:
Mrs. Olinski and The Souls have a special practice after tea at Sillington House. Mrs. Olinski relaxes as she talks with Mr. Singh about The Souls.

Characterization-Reaction Chart

Directions: By telling the reader what a character does, says, and thinks, and showing how he or she relates to other characters, a good writer can make fictional characters seem like real people. Sometimes, as we get to "know" the characters, our opinions of them change. As you read the novel, fill in the chart below. Under #1, jot down two examples of each character's actions. Under #2, tell why you think he/she acted that way. Under #3, explain how you would have reacted to the character if you had been there yourself.

	1. Says/Does	2. Why?	3. My Reaction
Noah			
Nadia			
Ethan			
Julian			

Vocabulary:

rendered 133	at random 133	stealth 133	pretext 134
grunges 134	contender 135	unprecedented 136	arrogance 136
caryatids 136	translucence 137	diversity 137	nanosecond 138
phalanx 138	reincarnation 142	incarnation 142	realm 143
Hecate's soul 143	Koran 145	Upanishads 145	

Discussion Questions and Activities:

1. Mr. LeDue said that if the Knightsbridge team lost, their coach would be hanged. Did the principal mean this "literally"? What is the difference between "literally" and "figuratively"? What rope was Mrs. Olinski referring to? *(page 134)*

2. Why was Dr. Rohmer worried? *(Pages 134-135, He was worried about his contract renewal, the district playoffs and the kind of embarrassing mistakes his deputy superintendent could make as master of ceremonies.)*

3. How did Mr. Fairbain embarrass the teachers and superintendent? *(Pages 136-137, He mispronounced Geronimo and asked Julian what his Indian tribe was.)* Why was this so awful?

4. How did The Souls know they won more than the championship over Knightsbridge School? *(Page 138, Michael Froelich and his pals put on their symbolic rope and then they also put one on Mrs. Olinski's van. The Souls knew that they not only had lifted Mrs. Olinski in her wheelchair in triumph, but they had helped give her the lift she needed with the class.)*

5. How do you think Mr. Singh knew about the question of why the academic team was chosen? Why do you think Mr. Singh is so grateful that Julian had been chosen? How long do you think it would have taken Julian to fit in if he had not become a part of The Souls? (pages 142-143)

Supplementary Activities:

1. Literary Analysis—Personification: Explain that personification is a figure of speech in which places, things, animals or ideas are endowed with human qualities. For example, page 145, "The dark wrapped the afternoon around her and kept it close."

   Ask: What is Mrs. Olinski saying about the way she perceives the dark? What feeling does this figure of speech lend?

2. Writing: Look for other examples of personification in the book. Try writing some of your own examples of personification.

- The dark was…
- The sky was…
- The woods…
- The wind…
- The flower…
- The mirror…
- The computer…

3. With a partner, write and record a song that gives the feeling of the novel.

Chapters 9, 10, 11, & 12—Pages 146-160

Chapter 9 Summary:
The commissioner with additional information gives the team credit for the acronym TIP. At the press conference Mr. Fairbain makes another big mistake by saying, "The taxpayers are very proud" when the announcer asks how the trip to Albany will be paid for. The tape of the press conference is sent to Florida to Century Village where the senior citizens decide to design and print T-shirts to sell for the bus fare.

Chapter 10 Summary:
The Souls triumph over their competition and they, along with Mrs. Olinski, receive the loving cup prize.

Chapter 11 Summary:
Mr. Singh tells Mrs. Olinski that all The Souls have returned from journeys on which they each found kindness in others and learned how to look for it in themselves. Mrs. Olinski realizes the kindness that The Souls have given her.

Chapter 12 Summary:
Mrs. Olinski asks "Did I choose you [The Souls], or did you choose me?" And The Souls answer, "Yes!"

Vocabulary:
photosynthesis 150   parched 153   frieze 153   perpetual 155

Discussion Questions and Activities:
1. How does Julian measure journeys? *(Page 151, He measures miles by quarter inches, oceans by cupfuls, and "learned to regard each port of call as part of the journey and not as destination.")* What did Mr. Singh mean when he said, "Every voyage begins when you do"?

2. Why was it easy for Julian to answer the last question in the contest about Humpty Dumpty? *(Page 76, He knew it was not in* Alice's Adventures in Wonderland *because*

he had studied that book for the invitations to the first tea, and thus he knew the answer had to be in Through the Looking Glass *by Lewis Carroll.)*

3. Why did Mrs. Olinski feel a sense of loss after The Souls had won? *(Page 155, Mr. Singh says she is missing future victories and the preparation and excitement.)* How did she act? What was Mr. Singh's advice to her? *(Page 156, "…put down anchor, look around, enjoy this port of call.")* What do you think he means? How could that apply to you after you have worked hard for something and then achieved it?

4. What journeys had each of The Souls made and what had each found? *(Pages 156-157, Noah at Century Village, Nadia on the Sargasso Sea, Ethan on the bus, and Julian on the cruise ships had found kindness.)*

5. What do you think the kindness of The Souls did for Mrs. Olinski? *(pages 159-160)*

6. How would you explain Mrs. Olinski's question, "Did I choose you, or did you choose me?" (page 160) The Souls answered, "Yes!" What did they mean?

Supplementary Activities:
1. Literary Analysis—Theme: Theme is an important idea that emerges from a story. Authors usually don't state the theme of a work outright, but let their readers decide for themselves what ideas in the story are the most important. For clues to theme, readers can look at the characters, the main events, and the conflicts in a story. You should also take a close look at what the main characters learn and how they change from the beginning of the story to the end. Most stories have several themes.

    With a small group, brainstorm some possible themes of *The View from Saturday*. The diagram below and the list on the next page should help you get started.

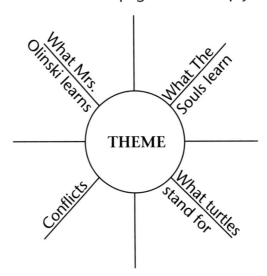

What issues did the author raise for you?

SOME UNIVERSAL
- coming of age
- courage
- family relationships
- kindness
- search for meaning
- values

2. Writing: After you have discussed theme with your group, decide for yourself what you think are the most important ideas in the story. Write a paragraph explaining your opinion.

3. Make a list of acronyms. (An acronym is a word formed by combining initial letters or syllables and letters of other words or of a series of words.)

Postreading Questions

1. Summarize the story using the story diagram below. What purpose is there in a story diagram? How would using a story diagram help an author?

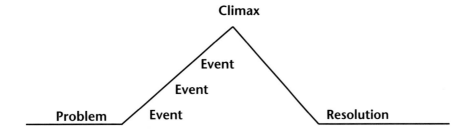

2. Characterization: Characters are developed by what they say, think, and do and by how others in the novel react to them. Review the attribute webs. Which character or characters provided wisdom and perspective? How did the characters change during the story? How would you explain the changes?

3. Plot: In literature the plot often is carried along by causes and effects of decisions made by the main characters. Had a character made an alternate decision, the plot would have turned in a different direction. What were the important decisions or turning points of this story?

4. Theme is the novel's central idea. What is this author's message? Why do you think the author wrote this story? What do you think is the most important thing to

remember about this story? Support your ideas for the theme or themes with examples from the novel. Is the central theme of this story presented directly or indirectly?

5. Do you notice anything unusual about the book's ending—or beginning?

6. Does the plot seem realistic? Were any events out of place or contrived? Did you find that any parts lost your attention? Would you change anything about this story? What would you say to the author about this book if you met her signing books in a bookstore?

7. What did you notice about Konigsburg's use of language?

8. If you were to place yourself in the book, who would you be and when would you enter?

9. If you were making a one hour video based on the story, which episodes would you include—and which would you leave out? Why?

10. Explain the significance of the title. What other titles could you think of for this novel?

Postreading Extension Activities

Writing Activities:
1. The theme is the author's main message. Think about the insights Mrs. Olinski has over the course of the novel. What do you think Konigsburg is saying about kindness?

2. Write a diary entry for one day that each of the main characters might write.

3. Pick one of the characters in the novel and write five questions that you would like to ask in order to understand the way he/she acted in the story.

4. Describe and analyze The Souls' relationship with their teacher, Mrs. Olinski. How was this relationship important in the novel?

5. Explain how Ethan or Julian change over the course of the novel. Include in your discussion any changes in behavior, appearance, self-confidence, and/or ideals as a result of the actions in the novel.

6. Add another chapter to the novel involving the same characters that would make the story more exciting.

7. How important is the setting to the story? (In what time and place is the story set?) How do the various settings contribute to the mood and move the plot along?

Describe the settings of *The View from Saturday* and how they are connected with the major ideas of the novel.

8. Conflict is structure that drives the plot. There are four main types: Man vs. Man, Man vs. Nature, Man vs. Society, and Inner Conflict. Analyze the main conflicts in *The View from Saturday*. Where do you find inner conflict? Which type of conflict would you say is most central to the story? Provide at least one example of each of the four types.

9. An epilogue is an addition to a story that tells what happened later. Choose a time in the future and write a brief epilogue to the activities of The Souls.

10. You are a TV script writer and you have been asked to create a series based on this novel. Write the outline for one episode taken from the novel.

11. Compare and contrast two of The Souls. How are these characters alike? What conflicts do they both face? How are they different? Use a Venn diagram to organize your thoughts.

12. Choose your own essay topic. (What do you notice about this story? What strikes you? What does this story remind you of? Can you relate to any of the characters or incidents?)

Listening and Speaking Activities:

1. Stage a TV interview with some of the central characters in the story. For homework, students playing each role gather impressions about what their character is like. Other students make lists of interview questions.

2. Retell an episode from your favorite chapter from the viewpoint of another character, e.g. Grandpa Nate or Allen Diamondstein.

3. Work with a partner to write an imaginary dialogue between yourself and one of the characters in the novel. The character you choose should act and respond in the same manner as he or she does in the novel. With your partner, present your dialogue for the class.

4. Pantomime a scene from the novel.

5. Make a list of occupations of people who make a living with their mouths. (Don't forget teachers.)

Language Study:

1. Collect examples of figurative language (metaphors, similes, personification) found through the book.

2. Make a list of Jewish or Yiddish terms and phrases in this story. How did you use context clues to help you figure out what these terms mean? What else did you do? How was the process of figuring out these terms similar to the way you figure out any word you don't know? Why didn't the author translate these words and phrases into English?

   (Teacher Note: The following is a list of Jewish or Yiddish words.)

   - Sha! a shanda far die kinder 8
   - pareve 11
   - chupah 17
   - mazel tov 17
   - hora 17
   - bubbe 26
   - zaftig 27
   - ruggelach 39
   - bobka 39

Art:

1. Draw a wedding picture of Margy and Grandpa Izzy, or a picture of them with the turtles.

2. Use charcoal, watercolor, or another medium to create a picture of a scene from the novel. Some suggestions: Allan trips over the wagon with the wedding cake; The Souls lift Mrs. Olinski and her wheelchair in the air.

3. Design a poster encouraging people to visit the area where the story takes place, e.g. Florida or New York State.

4. Draw a picture that shows the meaning of five vocabulary words.

5. Make a collage on a large piece of poster board. Divide the poster board into sections. Each section should represent a character in the story. You may use magazine cut-outs and drawings of your own.

Music:

Konigsburg tells several humorous anecdotes. Choose one and make it into a song. (You may choose to retell the story and set your words to a tune you know—such as "Darling Clementine"—or you may write your own tune.)

 # Teacher Information

Turtles:

Turtles are part of a large group of animals called reptiles. They are relatives of crocodiles, snakes, and lizards. They share some basic features. Although some spend a great deal of time in the water, they must breathe air. All reptiles have scaly or leathery skin. Reptiles have no built-in temperature control. When it is in the sun, a reptile's temperature will go up. When it is in the shade, a reptile's temperature will go down. This affects how and where reptiles will live and explains why turtles are more active on a hot day. They like to sunbathe to warm up their bodies.

Turtles are the only reptiles that have a shell. The female turtle does not give birth to a baby turtle; instead, she lays eggs. In each egg, a baby turtle grows until it is ready to hatch out of the egg and explore the world.

Turtles are found almost anywhere that it is warm for at least several months of the year. To survive winter, they hibernate. There are many different kinds of turtles, but they fall into the categories of: sea turtles, tortoises or land turtles, and freshwater turtles, sometimes called terrapins.

Sea turtles are found in the Atlantic and Pacific Oceans and in the Gulf of Mexico. Their legs are flattened, paddle-like flippers, and they spend almost all of their time in the water. They only come ashore to lay their eggs. Most sea turtles are very large. Many grow to be over 220 pounds.

Tortoises are turtles that can live only on land. They are poor swimmers and usually live near deserts and grasslands. They have stump-like legs and have high, rounded shells that are deeply patterned.

Freshwater turtles spend part of their time in the water of lakes, ponds and streams, and part of the time on land. They have many different styles of shells, usually flatter than the tortoise so that they can swim more easily. Their feet are usually suited for both walking and swimming. Most of these turtles have claws, and those that spend a great deal of time in the water have webbed feet.

Turtle shells may be brown or green all over, or a mottled mixture of dullish shades. Some may have brightly colored spots, streaks and borders, or intricate patterns. Whatever the shell looks like, it is bony and hard, and it is the turtle's main means of protection. This built-in armor may be one of the reasons that turtles have survived for so many generations.

The shell is made up of two parts, a top called the carapace, and a bottom called the plastron. The parts are usually joined at the sides by bony ridges. The front and back ends are openings through which the head, tail and legs stick out.

A turtle breathes through its mouth and nose and uses its lungs. The turtle's ribs cannot move to help it breathe, since they are affixed to the shell. However, the turtle can make its lungs expand by moving its legs. A swimming turtle uses up oxygen much faster than a resting one.

Assessment for *The View from Saturday*

Assessment is an on-going process, more than a quiz at the end of the book. Points may be added to show the level of achievement. When an item is completed, the teacher and the student check it.

Name _____ Date _____

Student   Teacher

_____ _____ 1. As you read, keep a Response Log. (See page 5 of this guide for suggested formats.)

_____ _____ 2. Write three questions about the novel and participate in a small group discussion of these and other student-generated questions.

_____ _____ 3. On chart paper, create a story map showing the character chapters in relation to the entire story.

_____ _____ 4. Do a small group dramatization of a scene in the story showing conflict.

_____ _____ 5. Assume the personae of the four students and write diary entries.

_____ _____ 6. Participate in a game where classmates try to guess which episode from the story you are drawing or pantomiming.

_____ _____ 7. After reading the novel, write an essay using one of the topics suggested in the Postreading Activities.

_____ _____ 8. Make a collage on a large piece of poster board. Divide the poster board into sections. Each section should represent a character in the story. You may use magazine cut-outs and drawings of your own.

_____ _____ 9. Alternative activity of your choice: _____

_____ _____ 10. Write a self-evaluation of your portfolio, explaining the strengths and weaknesses of various pieces, and assigning yourself an overall grade.

Note: For quizzes, tests, a study guide, and activity sheets focusing on critical thinking skills, vocabulary study, literary analysis, and writing skills, see the **Novel Units Student Packet** for *The View from Saturday*.